M000046511

The
Dittohead's
Guide to
Adult Beverages

The Dittohead's
Guide to
Adult Beverages

Britt Gillette

Since 1947
REGNERY
PUBLISHING, INC.
An Eagle Publishing Company • Washington, DC

Copyright © 2005 by Britt Gillette

All rights reserved. No part of this publication may be reproduced or transmitted in any form or by any means electronic or mechanical, including photocopy, recording, or any information storage and retrieval system now known or to be invented, without permission in writing from the publisher, except by a reviewer who wishes to quote brief passages in connection with a review written for inclusion in a magazine, newspaper, or broadcast.

Library of Congress Cataloging-in-Publication Data
Gillette, Britt.

The dittohead's guide to adult beverages / Britt Gillette.
p. cm.

Includes index.

ISBN 0-89526-012-3
1. Cocktails. 2. Beverages. I. Title.
 TX951.G479 2005
 641.8'74—dc22

                                    2005023030

Published in the United States by
Regnery Publishing, Inc.
One Massachusetts Avenue, NW
Washington, DC 20001
www.regnery.com

Distributed to the trade by
National Book Network
Lanham, MD 20706
Manufactured in the United States of America

1 0 9 8 7 6 5 4 3 2 1

Books are available in quantity for promotional or premium use. Write to
Director of Special Sales, Regnery Publishing, Inc., One Massachusetts
Avenue NW, Washington, DC 20001, for information on discounts and
terms or call (202) 216-0600.

To Rush Limbaugh, who saved at least one young skull full of mush before it could be brainwashed by the liberal establishment.

Contents

THE LIMBAUGH LEXICON

ADULT BEVERAGES Alcoholic beverages. Articulated in this classy way to avoid angering the parents of the youth of America who listen eagerly to *The Rush Limbaugh Show*.

AMERICA'S TRUTH DETECTOR Rush Limbaugh

BRECK GIRL Former senator and Democrat vice presidential candidate John Edwards, so named because of his beautiful, shiny, All-American Breck girl hair.

CALYPSO LOUIE Louis Farrakhan, current Nation of Islam leader and former calypso music singer who harbors a strange fascination with the number 19.

CLARENCE "THE FROGMAN" HENRY Rock-and-roll legend and personal friend of El Rushbo. His song "Ain't Got No Home" introduces Rush's Homeless Updates.

CLUB G'ITMO The U.S. military detention facility at Guantanamo Bay, Cuba, where terrorist detainees are fed orange-glazed chicken and rice pilaf and are provided imam-approved prayer rugs and air-conditioned jail cells.

CAMPI The preferred EIB plural form for "college campus." Home to a growing number of life-long dittoheads who irk their liberal brethren by challenging liberal beliefs, demanding true academic freedom, and hosting affirmative action bake sales.

COMMIE LIBS A subspecies of socialist in danger of extinction; many members are using their chameleon-like abilities to become environmentalist wackos.

DEFICIT SPENDING AWARENESS RIBBON A dittohead emblem made by folding a U.S. dollar into the shape of a ribbon. Pinning such a ribbon to one's lapel heightens public awareness of the ever-expanding federal budget deficit.

DEMOCRAT PARTY Not *Democratic*, as its leadership very rarely acts according to true democratic principles.

DER SCHLICK MEISTER Bill Clinton

DISGRONIFICATOR A nonexistent mechanism that an auto mechanic once told Rush was the cause of his car troubles. Rush believed him because the man had a statue of Jesus in his office.

DITTO This term developed as a timesaving greeting from listeners who would formerly waste valuable broadcast seconds praising Rush and his show. The *New York Times* has declared (accurately!) that "ditto" is shorthand for "You're wonderful, Rush, you're the best host I've ever heard. Don't ever go away." This does not mean—as some liberals erroneously charge—that listeners mindlessly say "ditto" to everything Rush says.

DITTOCAM Internet camera enabling Rush 24/7 members to view a live feed of Rush as he redefines greatness on the air

DITTOHEAD An avid listener of the EIB network

DOCTOR OF DEMOCRACY Rush Limbaugh, purveyor of American optimism

DOCUMENTED TO BE ALMOST ALWAYS RIGHT, 97.9% OF THE TIME The actual figure changes from time to time, as there are natural fluctuations in El Rushbo's accuracy. The rating is determined each month by an official Opinion Audit conducted by The Sullivan Group in Sacramento, California.

DOOM AND GLOOM The verbal byproduct of liberalism, most often propagated by Democrat politicians, partisan hacks in the liberal media, environmentalist wackos, and fringe kooks from the Hollywood Left.

DUBYA Affectionate nickname and term of reverence for George W. Bush

EIB Excellence in Broadcasting

ENVIRONMENTALIST WACKOS Fringe kookburgers not to be
confused with serious and responsible ecology-minded
people. Environmentalist wackos believe that mankind is
the greatest threat to nature, as opposed to being a part of
nature. They seek to destroy private property rights and
establish a socialist regime as a means of imposing their
nuttiness. Environmentalist wackos are frequently found
among the Hollywood Left, congressional staffers, and on
college campi that are hopefully nowhere near you.

FAIRNESS DOCTRINE First Amendment–trampling legislation
that liberal lawmakers hope to one day enact to effectively
eliminate talk radio (also known as the "Hush Rush Law").

FEMINAZI Widely misunderstood by most to simply mean
"feminist." Not so. A Feminazi is a feminist to whom
the most important thing in life is ensuring that as many
abortions as possible occur. There are fewer than
twenty-five known Feminazis in the United States today.

FREEPER A blogger on FreeRepublic.com, derided by the
liberal mainstream media for blowing the lid off various
liberal conspiracies.

FRUITED PLAIN America

GRAVITAS High seriousness. Used by countless partisan hacks in the liberal media during the 2000 presidential campaign to describe Dick Cheney.

GREAT MODERATES IN HISTORY A nonexistent history textbook often cited by Rush

HOMELESS OLYMPICS Future athletic event for homeless persons to be hosted in the California town of Rio Linda. Events will include such breathtaking displays of talent as synchronized panhandling, dumpster diving, and the shopping cart decathlon.

INFO-BABE Television journalists and commentators of the female persuasion who exhibit certain physical characteristics deemed desirable by society at large.

LIMBAUGH INSTITUTE FOR ADVANCED CONSERVATIVE STUDIES The award-winning, thrill-packed *Rush Limbaugh Show*

LIMBAUGH LETTER Rush's monthly newsletter

MILITANT VEGETARIANS Socialist wackos (not to be confused with docile, pacifist vegetarians who mind their own business) who see no difference between chicken factories and Nazi death camps.

NEW MATH An outcome-based educational concept whereby two plus two can equal five if such an assumption increases the self-esteem of the young skull full of mush who believes it.

PRESTIGIOUS ATTILA THE HUN CHAIR The senior position at the Limbaugh Institute for Advanced Conservative Studies, occupied by Rush Limbaugh. Named purposely to tweak and thwart leftist critics who complain that Rush is too far to the right.

RIO LINDA, CALIFORNIA A depressing, dreary neighborhood near Sacramento for which Rush has a soft spot in his heart. Known for having real-estate agents who despair of selling property there. Used to describe a place almost anyone would rather not be in. Most visible characteristic is that most homes have at least one car on concrete blocks in the front yard. These cars will serve as the Olympic Village when the first Annual Homeless Olympics are held in Rio Linda.

RONALD REAGAN Also known as Ronaldus Magnus. The best president in our lifetime, and a man unjustly maligned by liberals, environmentalist wackos, and all the aforementioned fringe groups.

SEASONED CITIZENS An increasingly large group of people demanding massive entitlements like free prescription drugs (such as Viagra) at the expense of their grandchildren.

SERVING HUMANITY Another way of describing Rush Limbaugh's incredible contribution to the human race.

TALENT ON LOAN FROM GOD Often misunderstood by hypercritical and sensitive types to mean Rush thinks he is God. On the contrary. Rush believes he is what he is because of the grace of God and that his time on earth, along with everyone's, is merely temporary.

THOUGHT POLICE The liberal arbiters of political correctness, so named for their uncanny resemblance to a group by the same name from George Orwell's dystopian novel *1984*.

UGLO-AMERICAN Rush was made aware that the term "ugly," when used to describe human beings, is insensitive, derogatory, and insulting. In a sincere effort to avoid offending anyone, he invented this new term, which he feels confident will be approved by the arbiters of what is politically correct. This term shows respect for this segment of society and does not strip them of their dignity.

＊All terms courtesy of www.rushlimbaugh.com

I

A TOAST TO HOLLYWOOD

ALEC'S *BON VOYAGE* BLACK AND TAN

Glass

A "National Lampoon's European Vacation" Souvenir German Stein

Ingredients

HALF PINT of Stout (imported from a sophisticated, nuanced European distributor)

HALF PINT of Lager (a beloved beverage among the French and German elite)

1 Empty Promise (Alec's brilliant thespian portrayal of Democrat politicians)

1 Leftist Hollywood Actor (how nice it would be if there really were just one)

Instructions

While addressing Martin Sheen as though he were truly the president of the United States (74% of Democrat voters polled believe that he is), combine the stout and lager in a

"National Lampoon's European Vacation" souvenir German stein, assuming it meets with United Nations approval following a "global taste test." Consume while waving goodbye to your favorite leftist actor, Alec Baldwin, as he sets sail for the socialist paradise of Europe.

Origin

This official farewell adult beverage is named in honor of noted Hollywood leftist Alec Baldwin, who claimed in 2000 that he would move to Europe if George W. Bush won the election.

Special Note

In the aftermath of the George W. Bush election victory (and re-election victory) and his subsequent 90% approval ratings, most Americans are still waiting for Alec Baldwin to fulfill his pre-election promise and leave the country for good. Apparently, Alec's promise was just B.S.—that's Barbra Streisand, for those of you in Rio Linda (another Hollywood leftist most Americans wish would move to Europe.)

OPRAH'S WHINE

Glass

A Giant "Whine" Glass

Ingredients

2 PARTS Gin (the correct spirit for getting in touch with one's inner spirit)

1 PART Grenadine (conducive to emotional female bonding)

A DASH of Light Cream (added in between free-flowing teardrops)

LOTS of Crying

Instructions

First, obtain tickets to the *Oprah Winfrey Show*, where you will be given a $30,000 car. Immediately afterward, start whining like a baby because Oprah didn't pay the taxes on the free car she gave you. When finished, combine ingredients in a giant "whine" glass, engage in an emotional outburst of uncontrolled sobbing while seeking sympathy from Dr. Phil for this obvious act of automobile tax victimization, and sip this adult beverage while crying profusely.

Origin

This adult beverage is named in honor of Oprah Winfrey, host of the *Oprah Winfrey Show*, a daily hour of nothing but constant weeping by guests, audience members, and the host herself. It is best consumed among friends while getting in touch with one's "inner-spirit" and "feel-gooded-ness."

Special Note

If you're a TV viewer who's grown to believe that over-emotional crying fits will bring world peace and/or that someone else is responsible for paying the taxes on your free car, do NOT panic. You have hope. First, stop whining and crying like a baby, stop watching the *Oprah Winfrey Show*, and get a grip on reality. Once you have done this, tune your radio to the EIB network (the only healthful addiction in America.) Listen three hours a day, five days a week, and within six months, you'll have the brand-new life you so ardently crave.

UGLO-AMERICAN COFFEE

Glass

A Collins Glass Bearing Michael Moore's Portrait

Ingredients

1 PART Whiskey (a "progressive" beverage that allows Uglo-Americans to consume it)

1 PART Irish Cream (due to its own history, sympathetic to Uglo-American discrimination)

3 PARTS Coffee (a widely beloved beverage, non-threatening to the Uglo-American lifestyle)

A SPLASH of Russo-Vodka (the universally agreed upon sensitive name for Russian vodka)

Instructions

While tearing up pictures of supermodels and movie stars who perpetuate unrealistic standards of physical beauty, combine ingredients in a Collins glass bearing the portrait of a prominent Uglo-American—Hollywood leftist filmmaker Michael Moore. Consume while lobbying your congressman for a special constitutional amendment that prohibits discrimination against Uglo-Americans.

Origin

This adult beverage is named in honor of those Americans deemed to be "ugly" by their fellow citizens. Given that such a word is insensitive, derogatory, and insulting, "Uglo-American" is the preferred alternative.

Special Warning:

According to the Surgeon General, extensive consumption of adult beverages has been shown to briefly transform even the most uglo of Uglo-Americans into individuals that society at large would deem either "studs" or "babes."

II

AS AMERICAN AS
AN APPLE MARTINI

HALLIBURTON'S DUBYA AND COKE

Glass

An Empty Pennzoil Bottle (a reminder of all that is evil in America)

Ingredients

1 PART Texas Whiskey (the kind consumed by filthy rich oil barons)

2 PARTS Cola (in truth, a byproduct of oil, further increasing Halliburton's obscene profits)

10 PARTS Conspiracy (no doubt insidiously linked to the Yale Skull & Bones society)

Instructions

While protesting George W. Bush's continued insistence on breathing (which he has yet to apologize for), combine ingredients in an empty Pennzoil bottle. Consume while accusing Bush of backing a manned mission to Mars in order to discover Martian oil fields that he and Halliburton can exploit for massive profits in their quest for domination of the solar system.

Origin

This adult beverage is named in honor of the most evil man in American history, George W. Bush, and his sinister relationship with the price-gouging big oil company Halliburton.

Special Note

George W. Bush liberates 20 million Iraqis, using Iraq's oil money to rebuild their nation as a freedom-loving democracy, and the liberal media claims he did it to increase profits at Halliburton. But when Algore sells off America's strategic petroleum reserve to Occidental Oil (a company in which he owns massive amounts of stock), that's simply part of his brilliant "reinventing government" program.

MORAL MODERATE MARTINI

Glass

To Be Determined (and even then you must keep an "open mind")

Ingredients

2 PARTS Watered-Down Gin (using straight gin is far too "radical")

1 PART Dry Vermouth (to offset the bland taste of sweet vermouth)

1 PART Sweet Vermouth (to offset the sharp taste of dry vermouth)

THE LYRICS to the "Moderate Fight Song" (now being rewritten in conference committee)

1 COPY of the Nonexistent Book *Great Moderates in History*

Instructions

While singing the "Moderate Fight Song" (being careful not to offend non-moderates) and calling for widespread "bipartisanship" (i.e. Republican submission to Democrat policies), combine ingredients in a mixing glass and stir. Next, look around the room to see what types of glasses other people are drinking from. Figure out which beverage container is the most popular and choose that one for your adult beverage. Consume while reading the nonexistent book *Great Moderates in History*, championed as the end-all book of virtue by the liberal mainstream media.

Origin

This adult beverage is named in honor of the self-proclaimed "moderates" across the Fruited Plain, who engage in the time-honored political tradition of waiting for the conventional wisdom to enjoy a safe majority on an issue and then bravely joining that majority.

Special Note

Unlike us lesser mortals, moderates possess a wisdom and virtue far surpassing that of the "reactionary radicals" on the far Left and Right (extremist kooks such as George Washington, Thomas Jefferson, Ben Franklin, Abe Lincoln, Teddy Roosevelt and Martin Luther King, Jr.) who actually take a position on an issue, believe in it, and stand up for it.

ENTITLE-MINT JULEP

Glass

Any Glass You've Taken from Someone Else (preferably a rich person)

Ingredients

1 PART Bourbon (procured by means of a monthly welfare check)

1 Mint Sprig (purchased with food stamps allocated for your 27 children)

SUGAR SYRUP (obtained via the "earned-income, sugar syrup tax credit)

MILLIONS of Government-Dependent Crybabies

Instructions

First, call your congressman and demand that each of the above ingredients be given to you free of charge as part of a new federal adult beverage entitlement program. Next, obtain a drinking glass that has been commandeered from someone else's private collection (preferably by the government). Finally, pour each of the federally mandated entitlement ingredients into the stolen glass. Consume while living off 13 extended weeks of unemployment checks while complaining that "the rich" don't pay "their fair share" of the nation's tax burden.

Origin

This adult beverage is named in honor of government largesse. According to Rush, our national symbol, the eagle, needs to be replaced by a huge sow that has a lot of teats and a bunch of fat little piglets hanging on them, all trying to suckle as much nourishment from them as possible.

Special Note

This space was reserved for a humorous comment, but that would require thought and effort on behalf of the author (who feels he is entitled to your purchase of this book whether you find it entertaining or not).

FUZZY NAVEL NEA

Glass

A National Education Association Coffee Mug (provided at taxpayer expense)

Ingredients

1 PART Vodka (or is it 3 parts? . . . wait, is it 7 parts?)

5 PARTS Peach Schnapps (or is it 4 parts?)

1 PART Orange Juice (hmm . . . maybe 3)

A TWIST of Orange Peel (or is it 2?)

1 COPY of the Book *Heather Has Two Mommies* (targeting young skulls full of mush)

Instructions

While attacking George W. Bush's Ted Kennedy–written trillion-dollar, big-government No Child Left Behind education bill as "not enough" simply because Bush proposed it, pour ingredients in an NEA coffee mug. (Remember that this adult beverage recipe was created by a dittohead using "old math," not "new math." Therefore, 2 parts equals 2 parts; 2 parts do not equal 5 parts, regardless of what this revelation may do to one's self-esteem). Consume while attempting to indoctrinate a group of kindergarten students by reading them *Heather Has Two Mommies*.

Origin

This adult beverage is named in honor of the National Education Association, a massive teacher's union that advocates such radical outcome-based education concepts as "new math"—in which 2 + 2=5 (or whatever the student wishes so as to encourage greater self-esteem)—and other policies that ultimately lead to the dumbing down of America's youth.

Special Note

Since 2 + 2=5 (or whatever else we wish), it stands to reason that two can also equal one. Therefore, in the interest of improving self-esteem, the NEA won't mind if we retitle its favorite book *Heather Has One Mommy*!

DISENFRANCHISED WHISKEY

Glass

An Empty Jack Daniel's Bottle (registered to vote in Florida as a Democrat)

Ingredients

3 PARTS Bourbon (part of a Republican conspiracy to get Democrat voters drunk)

2 PARTS Triple Sec (to commemorate Algore's failed Florida coup)

0 PARTS Dark Rum (which was too intimidated by Bush to turn out for this recipe)

1 EVIL Son-of-a-Bush Who Won't Allow the Election to Be Stolen

Instructions

While tossing sacks of George W. Bush votes into the ocean, combine ingredients in an empty Jack Daniel's bottle that was registered as a Democrat voter by a liberal 527 organization, and swirl gently. Consume while doing everything within your power to ensure that Jim Beam's vote is not thrown out by Dubya (that evil son-of-a-Bush who will do anything to grab the reins of power).

Origin

Designated an official dittohead adult beverage following the 2000 Florida recount, this recipe is named in honor of all the "disenfranchised" Democrats who voted for Pat Buchanan, couldn't remember their names at the polling place, or were so weak that the mere weight of their hands failed to penetrate the face of a ballot card.

Special Note

During November 2000, Algore frantically reiterated his belief that "every vote should be counted." And I'm sure if someone checks the voter roles in Florida, they'll find that Jim Beam voted for Algore—as did Jack Daniel, Captain Morgan, and Jose Cuervo.

RED, WHITE, & BLUE SHOOTER

Glass
A Shot Glass Displaying the American Flag

Ingredients

1 PART Grenadine (a thriving industry thanks to the long-term effect of the JFK tax cuts)

1 PART White Cream de Cacao (symbolizing the surrender of Japan and Germany)

1 PART Blue Curacao (symbolizing blue-state voters now in denial of their party's legacy)

1 Cigarette (FDR's tobacco product of choice—a definite modern-day no-no)

Instructions
While celebrating the presidency of America's first supply-side economics tax-cutter (JFK, not Ronald Reagan), layer each of the ingredients in a shot glass displaying the American flag—a symbol of FDR's pro-America stance, a position that today would kill his career as a Democrat politician. Consume while

wondering what the world would be like if only FDR had made an effort to "understand" the Japanese, rather than needlessly retaliating against them for some unknown, irrational reason.

Origin

This adult beverage is named in honor of America, known among dittoheads as The Fruited Plain, a majestic area once presided over by Democrat icons Franklin Delano Roosevelt and John F. Kennedy. Unfortunately, FDR was pro-America and JFK was both pro-America and pro–tax cut, which would today disqualify both men as Democrat presidential candidates.

Special Note

Wouldn't the world be better off today if FDR had conducted a "global test" before going to war with Japan? And how come that racist warmonger declared war on Germany, when we all know that Germany had nothing to do with the attack on Pearl Harbor? Meanwhile, Ted "The Swimmer" Kennedy wishes his brother had cut taxes on alcohol instead of income, a policy which would've saved him $42.6 million over the past forty years.

III

Rush to Excellence

SERVING HUMANITY HURRICANE

Glass

A "Limbaugh Institute for Advanced Conservative Studies" Coffee Mug

Ingredients

2 PARTS Rum (hated by liberals because it comprises more than its fair share of this recipe)

1 PART Lime Juice (squeezed by a freedom-loving, capitalist business enterprise)

1 PART Passionfruit Syrup (imported via Republican-enacted free trade policies)

1 Ashton Jamaica Leaf Cigar (purported to be a Rush favorite)

Instructions

While reading the latest issue of *Cigar Aficionado* (preferably with a Rush Limbaugh cover story), combine ingredients in an official "Limbaugh Institute for Advanced Conservative Studies" coffee mug. Consume along with an Ashton Jamaica leaf cigar while watching the Doctor of Democracy have more fun than a human being should be allowed to have on the Rush 24/7 dittocam.

Origin

This adult beverage is named in honor of Rush Limbaugh, the epitome of moral virtue, a man who says more in five seconds than most talk-show hosts say in an entire show, and a man serving humanity on a daily basis with talent on loan from God.

Special Note to Liberals

Much to your chagrin—no matter how much you would like to reinstitute the Fairness Doctrine— America's Truth Detector will continue to redefine greatness on the radio with half his brain tied behind his back (just to make it even) until every last person in America agrees with him!

KFBK SACRAMENTO SCOTCH

Glass

Any Glass Embossed with a Picture of a Pre-1983 Adult Beverage Disgronificator

Ingredients

2 PARTS Scotch (consumed in celebration of Rush taking his show national)

3 PARTS Club Soda (not made from clubs, for those of you in Rio Linda)

1 PART Lemon Juice (juice from lemons, for those of you in Rio Linda)

A SPLASH of Grenadine (suggested for this recipe by the devil himself)

1 Rush Limbaugh Power Tie

1 Post-1983 Turntable with a Disgronificator

Instructions

While wearing your Rush Limbaugh power tie, combine

ingredients in any glass embossed with a picture of a pre-1983 adult beverage disgronificator (which, while imbibed and walking backward, allows you to hear the devil's voice). Consume while perched on the cutting edge of societal evolution.

Origin

This adult beverage is named in honor of the radio station KFBK in Sacramento, California, where Rush Limbaugh perfected his formula for a successful national talk radio show. He informed his audience that they could hear the devil speak if they played Slim Whitman's "Una Paloma Blanca" backwards on a turntable with a pre-1983 "disgronificator" (a nonexistent mechanism that an auto mechanic once told Rush was the cause of his car troubles).

Special Note

It has been brought to my attention that if one reads this book backwards using a special text version of the disgronificator, he will get Hillary Clinton's talking points for the 2008 campaign!

EL RUSHBO

Glass

A Highball Glass Emblazoned with the EIB Network Logo

Ingredients

1 PART Rum (shares the first two letters of its name with Rush)

2 PARTS Blue Gatorade (consumed while playing a round of golf in honor of Rush)

2 PARTS Sprite (in recognition of capitalist lemon-lime soda companies)

1 Prestigious Attila the Hun Chair (symbolic of complete radio industry dominance)

TALENT on Loan from God (why liberals don't stand a chance against El Rushbo)

Instructions

Utilizing talent on loan from God (assuming that, unlike most liberals, you acknowledge the existence of God), combine ingredients in a highball glass emblazoned with the EIB logo and top off with whipped cream (but please use the whipped cream in this adult beverage recipe the way Rush would use it and not in the manner in which Bill Clinton would use it). Enjoy from the comfortable confines of your own Attila the Hun chair, the undisputed seat of talk-radio industry power.

Origin

This dittohead adult beverage is affectionately named in honor of Rush Limbaugh—lover of mankind, protector of motherhood, supporter of fatherhood (in most instances), general all-around good guy, and a man designated by the U.S. Department of Education as a bona fide "weapon of mass instruction."

Special Note

This adult beverage is documented to almost always taste great, 96.712 percent of the time, just as El Rushbo is documented to be almost always right, 97.963 percent of the time.

EIB ECSTASY ELIXIR

Glass

A Palm Beach County Coconut Shell (from the home of the EIB southern command)

Ingredients

2 PARTS Malibu Rum (in honor of the California beach town infested with leftist kooks)

1 PART Coconut Cream (an organic, all-natural favorite of environmentalist wackos)

2 PARTS Crushed Peaches (harmless little fuzzballs—just like Rush)

1 COPY of *See, I Told You So*

THE MOST Contagious Infection Known to Man (EIB—for which no known cure exists)

Instructions

While reading Rush Limbaugh's book *See, I Told You So* (the epitome of excellence in tomes of political commentary), combine ingredients in a Palm Beach County coconut shell and consume while standing outside El Rushbo's $24 million Palm Beach estate (which the liberal media loathes but free enterprise–loving dittoheads celebrate).

Origin

This adult beverage is named in honor of EIB, an airborne phenomenon spread by casual contact. Currently, no known cure exists for those who have contracted EIB, because EIB is itself a cure. Therefore, it is best not to fight it, but rather to enjoy it. To properly amplify the EIB infection, try consuming this delicious adult beverage while immersed in the intoxicating airwaves of America's Truth Detector.

Special Note

Following consumption of this adult beverage, you may feel the need to lie down and take a nap. It is your employer's responsibility to provide you with a proper napping space. However, if you can not locate one (or if it fails to meet proper OSHA standards), then feel free to use the Rush 24/7 Nap Room at www.rushlimbaugh.com.

RIO LINDA ROUSER

Glass

A Bottle Found in the Gutter (litter from the Homeless Olympics)

Ingredients

1 PART Brandy (wrapped in a brown paper bag so as to resemble a vagrant's beverage)

1 PART Blackberry Liqueur (obtained from a homeless man's personal collection)

1 PART Cranberry Juice (from a half-empty bottle found in a back alley dumpster)

1 DVD of "First Annual Homeless Olympics" Highlights (for pure entertainment)

1 "First Annual Homeless Olympics" T-Shirt (to express support for homeless athletes)

Instructions

While viewing the highly competitive panhandling events on your limited-edition "First Annual Homeless Olympics"

DVD, combine ingredients in a discarded bottle you found in the gutter (for those of you in Rio Linda, gutters are those continuous slabs of concrete outlining the asphalt roadways). Consume while wearing your "First Annual Homeless Olympics" T-shirt.

Origin

This adult beverage is named in honor of Rio Linda, California—a slightly backward neighborhood near Sacramento for which Rush harbors a soft spot in his heart. The most notable characteristic of loveable Rio Linda is that most homes have at least one car on concrete blocks in the front yard. According to Rush, these cars will serve as the Olympic Village when the First Annual Homeless Olympics are held in Rio Linda.

Special Note

In the mid-1980s, a radio station in Rio Linda cancelled Rush's show because it did not match "the intellectual standards of the community."

BAKE SALE BREEZE

Glass

A Fort Collins, Colorado, Souvenir Collins Glass (purchased at Dan's Bake Sale)

Ingredients

1 PART Apricot Brandy (purchased from a local church brandy sale)

1 PART Banana Liqueur (a fascinating entrepreneurial innovation utilizing bananas)

2 PARTS Orange Juice (in honor of the first entrepreneur to carton and sell orange juice)

1 Man Trying to Earn the Cash for a *Limbaugh Letter* Subscription

Instructions

While reading your own personal copy of *The Limbaugh Letter*, combine ingredients in a Fort Collins, Colorado, souvenir Collins glass. Consume while celebrating the entrepreneurial American spirit (much to the chagrin of liberal Democrats everywhere) with millions of dittoheads across the Fruited Plain.

Origin

This adult beverage is named in honor of Dan's Bake Sale, also known as Rushstock '93. In May 1993, some 65,000 dittoheads flocked to Fort Collins, Colorado, to support one listener's quest to earn the money for a *Limbaugh Letter* subscription fee by hosting a bake sale. As CBS News reported (much to Dan Rather's disappointment), "The spectacle was enough to drive a stake through the heart of liberalism."

Special Note

If you are a parent, then you may find that your "chil'ren" want to host a bake sale of their own in an effort to raise funds for paying down the national debt. If so, rest assured (precedent acts as a guide here) that Bill Clinton will be more than willing to accept the money of these well-intentioned yoots (proper EIB pronunciation of "youths") of America.

IV

DRINK ONE
FOR THE GIPPER

FREE ENTERPRISE EYE-OPENER

Glass

Any Sour Glass Bought with a Tax Refund (i.e. *your own* money)

Ingredients

2 PARTS Light Rum (in honor of the tax-cutter, JFK—the original, not John F-ing Kerry)

1 PART Triple Sec (a delicious adult beverage component created by entrepreneurs)

A DASH of Pernod (a delightful product of free enterprise)

A DASH of Irish Cream (in honor of Ronald Reagan's Irish heritage)

1 Egg Yolk (produced on a capitalist farm)

A DASH of Superfine Sugar (harvested by rugged individualist sugar cane plantation owners)

Instructions

At a celebration honoring Ronald Reagan (most likely to be found in a "red state"), combine ingredients in a shaker half-filled with ice cubes and shake well. Strain into a glass purchased with some extra money you have following the Bush tax cuts.

Origin

This adult beverage is named in honor of the entire free-enterprise system and that sacred moment when zero-sum liberals realize the real-world mechanics of a free market economy.

Special Note

For an example of a bold entrepreneurial endeavor, one need look no further than the pages of this book — an intentional and blatant slap in the face of liberal government jobs programs and a purely self-interested attempt on behalf of the author to avoid participation in future recessions.

THE PREGNANT CHAD

Glass

An Empty Florida Orange Juice Carton

Ingredients

2 PARTS Rum (a possible cause of Democrat ineptitude in the voting booth)

2 PARTS Unsweetened Pineapple Juice (approved by a United Nations election observer)

2 DASHES Angostura Bitters (indicative of liberal bitterness)

A DASH of Pernod (for the strength to punch all the way through the ballot)

1 PART Ginger Ale (a favorite of liberal seasoned citizens who voted for Pat Buchanan)

1 Stork Yard Sign Reading: "It's a Gore!"

Instructions

While suing the state elections board for allowing Ralph Nader on the ballot, despite your contention that every voter should be heard, combine ingredients in a shaker and pour into the empty orange juice carton. Place the stork yard sign in your front yard, and slurp through a straw while holding your ballot up to the light.

Origin

This adult beverage is named in honor of Vice Perpetrator Algore's endless litigation and failed coup attempt following George W. Bush's 2000 Florida election victory.

Special Warning for Democrats

Abstinence is the only 100% effective guard against a pregnant chad. Therefore, it is recommended for your own safety that you refrain from voting in all future elections.

EVIL EMPIRE ERASER

Glass

An American Flag Shot Glass

Ingredients

2 PARTS Vodka (now abundantly available in the Russian free
market economy)

2 PARTS Kahlua (purchased during the Carter years as a hedge
against inflation)

1 PART Tonic Water (salvaged from the rubble of the Berlin Wall)

Ronald Reagan (the greatest president in the history of
the universe)

Instructions

While watching liberals cringe at the
phrase "axis of evil" in the same manner in which they cringed at the phrase
"evil empire," combine ingredients in
an American flag shot glass and shoot
while laughing hysterically at the lib-

eral media's feeble attempts to give credit for the Soviet demise to Jimmy Carter and modern liberalism.

Origin

This adult beverage is named in honor of former president Ronald Reagan, who won the Cold War by defeating the "evil empire" known as the Soviet Union (despite the liberal contention that Reagan's victory resulted from policies put in place by the great peanut farmer, Jimmy Carter).

Special Note

Now that an entire decade has passed, we conservatives must finally admit the truth: The Soviet Union collapsed because of Jimmy Carter's secret plan to appear weak and incompetent, thus lulling Communist Russia into a deep sleep (a.k.a. an evil malaise), at which time the liberal-sponsored Global Peace March for Nuclear Disarmament dealt a mighty death blow to the heart of Soviet imperialism!

SELF-RELIANCE SNOW CONE

Glass

A Hand-Carved Wooden Drinking Cup

Ingredients

1 PART Vodka (created by a fellow self-reliant business owner)

2 PARTS Milk (extracted from a cow with your own bare hands)

1 PART Butterscotch Schnapps (purchased with actual earned income)

A SPLASH of Cinnamon Schnapps (ditto)

0 Government Jobs Programs

1 Entrepreneurial, Can-Do, Rugged Individualist

Instructions

First, you need a drinking cup. So, using your pioneer instincts, cut down a tree with your bare hands. Fashioning a crude tool from a rock, carve an ornate drinking cup from the fallen wood. Since it's illegal to distill your own liquor, carve additional relics from the fallen tree and sell them at a craft show in order to raise the necessary funds to purchase the ingredients for this adult beverage. Line your carved drinking cup with ice, add ingredients, and consume while being proud that you didn't need any government assistance to produce your own adult beverage.

Origin

This adult beverage is named in honor of self-reliant, rugged individualists across the Fruited Plain. Often, such people are known as entrepreneurs and small businessmen, and they are more likely to be found in those states identified as "Bush Country."

Special Note

Unfortunately, liberal "girly-man" Democrats can not stand the taste of this adult beverage. Its manufacture requires no input from big-government bureaucracy, and the individual who mixes it has no incentive to see liberal Democrats entrenched in office for all eternity.

TAXING THE POOR

Glass

A Used Fast-Food Soda Cup

Ingredients

1 PART Apple Vodka (heavily taxed so as to burden the poor)

2 PARTS Apple Juice (purchased by selling food stamps on the street for 50 cents on the dollar)

A DASH of Grenadine (ripped from the hands of a seasoned citizen by Republican street thugs)

1 Maraschino Cherry (stolen from a poor child's mouth)

1 Sinister, Evil Laugh

Instructions

While finalizing your plans to heap further destruction and misery on the nation's poor (a unified conspiracy involving Republicans, Darth Vader, Dr. Evil, and Satan), mix ingredients in a cocktail shaker and garnish with a maraschino cherry. Complement consumption of this adult beverage with a noticeably sinister and evil laugh directed at the poor—especially hapless children and elderly seasoned citizens.

Origin

This adult beverage is named in honor of a brilliant idea for eliminating the national debt—raising taxes on the poor. Originally, Rush offered up this suggestion on April Fool's Day, but liberals took it seriously and were offended anyway.

Special Note

If Democrats are going to blame Republicans for targeting the poor, then we may as well tax the hell out of them!

HOMELESS HIGHBALL

Glass

An Empty Malt Liquor Bottle (concealed in a brown paper bag)

Ingredients

1 PART Whiskey (a popular adult beverage among America's homeless population)

2 PARTS Ginger Ale (salvaged while rummaging through a restaurant dumpster)

Clarence "The Frogman" Henry's "Ain't Got No Home" (The Homeless Update Theme)

Instructions

While outfitting your luxurious 22-square-foot cardboard box with central air and heating (a big step up from your old park bench), combine ingredients in an empty malt liquor bottle brilliantly concealed from authorities in a brown paper bag, and shake well. Consume in memory of all the homeless personally assaulted and murdered by Ronald

Reagan (who would sneak out of the White House at night and steal shopping carts, blankets, and cans of beans from the "temporarily abode-less").

Origin
This adult beverage was created to serve as an eternal monument to the memory of the billions-upon-billions of homeless who perished during the decade of greed and the eight-year regime of American dictator Ronaldus Magnus.

Special Note

Amazingly, after an eight-year hiatus during the Clinton administration, the billions of homeless rotting in our urban gutters have returned. This is, of course, attributable to the presidency of George W. Bush.

V

 DRINK TILL
THESE MAKE SENSE

A DOSE OF DOOM & GLOOM

Glass

An Empty Poison Bottle

Ingredients

1 PART Gin (consumed by 18-year-olds recently drafted by the evil Bush administration)

2 PARTS Triple Sec (laced with cyanide now that Bush is president)

4 PARTS Orange Juice (unavailable because of all the hurricanes Bush unleashed on Florida)

Instructions

While addressing a room of handicapped minority lesbians, accuse Republicans of a unified conspiracy to eliminate wheelchair ramps, bring back Jim Crow laws, and force lesbians to wear a scarlet "L" in public. Then combine ingredients in an empty poison bottle symbolic of George W. Bush's evil intentions for America. Consume while telling seasoned citizens that they'll be kicked into the gutter if Republicans

ever get into power, conveniently forgetting that Republicans are already in power.

Origin

This adult beverage is named in honor of
the perpetual avalanche of doom and
gloom emanating from the mouths of liberal Democrats. These Democrats view
America as a giant, never-ending soup line
filled with homophobic racists who reside solely in "red
states."

Special Warning

Liberal doom and gloom, also known among dittoheads as a "created crisis," takes many forms, such as
the "campaign finance crisis," "the prescription drug
crisis," "the George W. Bush arsenic in the water crisis," and other such Barbra Streisand (that's B.S., for
those of you in Rio Linda) manufactured for the
express purpose of imposing the liberal agenda on an
unwilling and unsuspecting American public.

SEASONED CITIZEN SANGAREE

Glass

An Aluminum Can Found in a Ditch (to be cashed in for prescription drugs)

Ingredients

1 PART Tawny Port (now fully covered by the Medicare free prescription drug program)

2 PARTS Whiskey (provided free to even the wealthiest of seasoned citizens)

1 PART Club Soda (for washing down free prescription drugs)

ENDLESS Democratic Demagoguery of Social Security

MILLIONS of Grandparents Voting to Screw Their Grandchildren

Instructions

While cowering at the thought of evil Republicans stealing your Social Security money, combine ingredients in an aluminum can you found while combing the highway for soda cans to cash in to pay for your ridiculously high-priced prescription drugs. Swirl the can, and consume while demanding that every expense in your daily life be paid for by someone else simply because you've reached a certain age.

Origin

This adult beverage is named in honor of the seasoned citizens of America, an increasingly large group of people demanding massive entitlements like free prescription drugs (such as Viagra) at their grandchildren's expense.

Special Note

Please send a few spare dollars to Dick Gephardt's mother, a woman who, according to Dick, is languishing in poverty and can ill afford food, much less her own prescription drugs (despite her son's yearly $180,000 salary.)

AFFIRMATIVE ACTION AMBROSIA

Glass

A Measuring Cup (to ensure precise fulfillment of quotas)

Ingredients

0 PARTS Light Rum (using light rum is insensitive to minority rums)

3 PARTS Dark Rum (to rectify the past injustice of rampant light rum preferences)

3 PARTS Soda (cola is preferred over a lighter soda, such as Sprite)

QUOTAS That Aren't "Quotas" (except that they really are quotas)

Instructions

While throwing an "affirmative action bake sale" on a local college campus, or campi (the preferred EIB plural form for those of you in Rio Linda), combine ingredients in a measuring cup. Consume while labeling as "racist" any of your friends or companions who dare to add light rum to their favorite adult beverages.

Origin

This adult beverage is named in honor of government-sanctioned discrimination. Make sure that you don't add light rum to this adult beverage when dark rum is available instead. Failure to do so may result in court-ordered sensitivity training.

Special Note

A firm supporter of government-sanctioned discrimination, the NAALCP (National Association for the Advancement of *Liberal* Colored People) dreams of the day when prohibition will be re-instituted in America—with only "light" rum banished from the shores of the United States.

BUREAUCRACY BOURBON PUNCH

Glass

A Coffee Mug Fully Compliant with OSHA, FDA, and EPA Standards

Ingredients

1 PART Bourbon (purchased in a controlled, regulated, government-sanctioned environment)

2 PARTS Triple Sec (produced and price-controlled as the result of a federal mandate)

4 PARTS Grapefruit Juice (made by subsidized farmers paid not to grow cantaloupe)

1 PART Fruit Punch (sold to children following intense scrutiny of its advertising methods)

1 Cigarette (ceding vast tax revenues to big government)

Instructions

While filling out Form X27, Section 45Q, Subsection 19-A2, Chapter S91 in order to comply with tax regulations for your child's cardboard box lemonade stand, combine ingredients (assuming they're fully compliant with all federal regulations —

especially the Department of Energy's EW-57, directive A) in a coffee mug (designed in compliance with standards of the Department of Weights and Measures). Consume while smoking a cigarette outside, maintaining a safe distance of no less than 27.5 yards from any non-smoking individual, while standing on your head with your left shoe untied to comply with FDA executive orders 67A, 48V, paragraphs J and Y.

Origin

This adult beverage is named in honor of liberal-created big-government bureaucracy.

Special Note

What if the Ten Commandments had been written by a government bureaucrat? "Thou shall not murder" would have been "Thou shall not, with deference to the following stated exceptions (see paragraphs A26 & Q67, subsection B, enumerated clause #33), under any circumstance (unless otherwise contrary to the regulations outlined in EPA, FDA, CBO, or OSHA congressional directives) take a life (herein defined as a fully functional non-fetus operating within the world for no fewer than 47 minutes without medical assistance) in a manner unpleasing to Almighty God (herein defined as the federal government).

DEFICIT DAIQUIRI

Glass

A $792 Dixie Cup (the inevitable byproduct of federal bureaucracy)

Ingredients

1 PART Rum (from a federal study examining a link between rum and crop circles)

1 PART Grapefruit Juice (purchased at an unnecessary premium due to extensive farm subsidies)

1 PART Cranberry Juice (from an EPA-approved juice factory powered by cow manure)

1 Lime Wedge (harvested by liberal-approved laborers paid a "fair" living wage)

1 Deficit Spending Awareness Ribbon

Instructions

While attending a candlelight vigil in front of the Times Square national debt clock, combine ingredients in a $792

Dixie cup purchased by the federal government. Garnish with a lime wedge, and consume while wearing a "deficit spending awareness" ribbon to illustrate your "awareness" of the deficit.

Origin

This adult beverage is named in honor of the deficit spending awareness ribbon, a dittohead emblem that serves to heighten awareness of the ever-expanding federal budget deficit. (This ribbon is also known among liberals as "the solution to the deficit," as wearing themed ribbons is the answer to all the world's problems.)

Special Note

Just like AIDS, the federal budget deficit could be forever eliminated if we would simply heighten "awareness" of its existence by wearing ribbons and hosting candlelight vigils that show we "care."

DNC LONG ISLAND ICED TEA

Glass

A Chalice from a Buddhist Temple

Ingredients

1 PART Vodka (a gift from Russian oligarchs fascinated with American democracy)

1 PART Triple Sec (from the nightstand of the Lincoln Bedroom)

1 PART Tequila (a gift from a wealthy, mysterious Indonesian banker)

1 PART Rum (a campaign contribution from "big rum" lobbyists)

1 PART Gin (bartered in exchange for secret missile technology)

1 PART Sour Mix (a gift from Democrat donors sour about eight years of GOP rule)

Instructions

While attending a Tupperware party to raise money for those in need of charity (i.e. the Democrat Party), combine ingredients in a chalice commandeered from a Buddhist temple (compliments of a trademark Algore fund-raiser). Consume while handing out presidential pardons to anyone who donated so much as twelve cents and a piece of lint to your reelection effort.

Origin

This adult beverage is named in honor of the innumerable illegal and hilarious ways in which Democrats and the Democratic National Committee raise money for political campaigns.

Special Note

George W. Bush once described Bill Clinton's presidency as "so much promise to no great purpose," and Clinton would probably agree. If he could travel back in time, he wouldn't just rent out the Lincoln Bedroom, but also the Blue Room, the East Room, the Oval Office, the whole West Wing, the Rose Garden, and his own bedroom—maybe even Hillary's bedroom too! (Does $500,000 for a trip on Marine One sound fair?)

JESSE JACKSON'S GIN AND JUICE

Glass
A Rainbow/PUSH Collection Jar

Ingredients

2 PARTS Gin (takes the edge off after a long day of attacking Republicans)

3 PARTS Orange Juice (provides strength for juggling wives and mistresses)

3 PARTS Apple Juice (a source of vitamins for the child of your pregnant mistress)

Instructions
While listening to a replay of Jesse Jackson's inspiring 2000 Democrat National Convention speech, titled "Get Out Da Bushes"—a speech that, to some, rivaled Martin Luther King, Jr.'s "I Have A Dream," the Gettysburg Address, and the Sermon on the Mount—combine ingredients in a Rainbow/PUSH coalition collection jar. Consume while telling your followers

that Republicans (conspirators who made the black jelly bean the worst-tasting candy in the world) want to kill old people, burn black churches, and return to the days of slavery.

Origin

This adult beverage is named in honor of The . . . Reverend . . . Jesse . . . Jackson . . . (his name must be pronounced in a reverent near-whisper), purveyor of racially divisive rhetoric and proponenet of class warfare in America.

Special Note

Does your town harbor a misunderstood 19-year-old kindergarten student, wrongfully expelled for knifing his teacher? Has your town been singled out in an obvious act of racial prejudice by a flash flood or tornado? There's no need to worry: For no charge at all (except a small donation), Jesse Jackson will magically appear and orchestrate your protest for you!

CORE BELIEF BOOMERANG

Glass

Whichever Glass Is Most Popular Right This Second

Ingredients

1 PART Gin (unless criticized, in which case, switch to rum or some other liquor)

1 PART Dry Vermouth (or you could use sweet vermouth or nothing at all)

A DASH of Bitters (or maybe sugar...what do the polls say?)

A SPLASH of Maraschino Liqueur (or whatever else you want)

Paul Shonklin's Musical Parody "Algore Paradise"

Instructions

While being for gay marriage, then against gay marriage, then for partial gay marriage (before finally settling on a policy of civil unions for handicapped immigrant lesbians), pour ingredients into whichever glass Dick Morris assures you is the most popular right this very second.

However, if anyone expresses the slightest disapproval at your selection, immediately backpedal and refuse to tell anyone what type of glass you're using. Consume alongside anti-smoking activist Algore while helping him harvest his tobacco fields.

Origin

This adult beverage is named in honor of the ever-vacillating, poll-dependent behavior of numerous liberal Democrats in constant search of their "core beliefs."

Special Note

John F-ing Kerry, Bill Clinton, and their Democrat friends change views so often to coincide with public opinion that it's only a matter of time before they're full-fledged Reaganite conservatives! (Although, their conversion will probably only last a day or two.)

SANDY BURGLAR SHOOTER

Glass

A Souvenir Shot Glass Stolen from the National Archives (stuffed in your socks)

Ingredients

1 PART Tequila (from a stolen bottle stuffed in your pants)

1 PART Triple Sec (from a flask hidden in your sock)

1 LIME Wedge (inadvertently hidden under files in your briefcase)

0 Self-Incriminating Documents (shredded by the disorganized Sandy Burglar)

Instructions

Any of the above ingredients may be added to or subtracted from this recipe "inadvertently," or if you wish, you can tear out this page, stuff it in your pants, and pretend it never existed. But if you want to acknowledge the existence of this recipe, combine the ingredients in a souvenir shot glass stolen from the National Archives. Make one for your pal Bill Clinton and shoot while the two of you laugh at how disorganized and incompetent you are.

Origin

This adult beverage is named in honor of former national security adviser Sandy Berger, caught by National Archive employees while "inadvertently" stuffing classified Clinton-era national security documents into his socks and pants.

⚠

Special Warning

Now children across the globe have a new excuse for their teachers: "Sandy Berger stole my homework!"

"THOUGHT POLICE" PUNCH

Glass

A Collins Glass Inscribed with the Year *1984*

Ingredients

2 PARTS Gin (criticism of which guarantees that you'll be branded a hard-hearted liquor bigot)

3 PARTS Grape Juice (to be criticized under no circumstances whatsoever, you grapeophobe)

100 PARTS Liberal Double-Speak (example "victory"="quagmire")

Instructions

Combine ingredients in a Collins glass inscribed with the year *1984*, assuming it's purchased from a store owned by gay, flag-burning Wiccans supplied by a minority lesbian no-bid government contract (and if you don't buy from such a store, you're clearly a racist bigot). Enjoy while making sure you don't say anything that can possibly be deemed "offensive" by any segment of a protected class or perceived group of minority victims (in other words, anyone but heterosexual white males).

Origin

This adult beverage is named in honor of the liberal arbiters of political correctness, also known among dittoheads as "the thought police" for their uncanny resemblance to a group by the same name from George Orwell's dystopian novel *1984*.

Special Note

While consuming this adult beverage, it's probably not a good idea to point out that Donavan McNabb is overrated, even if he wins one of three spots on the NFC Pro Bowl roster after compiling a quarterback rating of 79.6, which ranks ninth in his conference and sixteenth in the NFL.

NEW DEMOCRAT NEXUS

Glass

A "Bush Country Red" Coffee Mug

Ingredients

1 PART Gin (from any bar found in a trendy Ivy League bastion of intellectualism)

2 PARTS Red Kool-Aid (for all the gun-loving, homophobic, Bible-belt hicks)

1 PART Blue Kool-Aid (for all the intellectually superior blue-state sophisticates)

Instructions

In an effort to trick red-state voters, participate in a staged duck hunt with a camouflaged John F-ing Kerry (even though true hunters wear fluorescent orange so as not to get shot), then combine ingredients in a "Bush Country Red" coffee mug. Consume while Kerry declares himself president-elect

of the newly seceded Blue States of America and appoints
Zell Miller chief architect of the new "spitball" division of
the U.S. Armed Forces.

Origin

This adult beverage is named in honor of liberal political
candidates who masquerade as "New Democrats" (i.e. conservatives) during election season. These imposters frequently use the word "values" whenever they speak, in a
transparent attempt to trick mainstream Americans (i.e., the
very voters they despise as Jesus-loving, Confederate
flag–waving, inbred redneck hicks) into voting for them.

Special Note

Please take a moment of silence to recognize the gut-
wrenching hardship experienced by John Kerry voters
suffering from Post-Election Selection Trauma (PEST).
These blue-state PESTs are victims of a Karl Rove
election thievery designed to screw Democrats. How
else could all those mainstream media exit polls and
liberal pundits have been wrong?

CALYPSO LOUIE

Glass

A Souvenir Nation of Islam Coffee Cup

Ingredients

6 PARTS Kahlua (using Farrakhan math, this translates into "600,000 Parts Kahlua")

6 PARTS Amaretto (a word with 8 letters—you add 11, and you get 19!)

19 PARTS Orange Juice (two words with 11 letters—you add 8, and you get 19!)

7 SPLASHES of Spiced Rum (if possible, this further confuses Farrakhan followers)

100,000 Confused Followers

Instructions

Add 6 parts Kahlua, 6 parts Amaretto, and 7 splashes of spiced rum to a souvenir Nation of Islam coffee cup, and marvel at the fact that 6 + 6 + 7 equals 19! Mix with orange juice, stir slowly, and watch while guilty white liberals in the mainstream media fawn all over yet another self-proclaimed liberal black leader, whose "Million Man March" had about 100,000 attendees.

Origin

This adult beverage is named in honor of Louis Farrakhan, former calypso singer and current Nation of Islam leader, who for some unknown reason harbors a strange conspiratorial fascination with the number 19.

> "Abraham Lincoln, the sixteenth president. Thomas Jefferson, the third president, and 16 and three make 19 again. What is so deep about this number 19? Why are we standing on the Capitol steps today? That number 19—when you have a nine you have a womb that is pregnant. And when you have a one standing by the nine, it means that there's something secret that has to be unfolded."
>
> —THE HONORABLE MINISTER LOUIS FARRAKHAN

VI

FROM RONALDUS MAGNUS
TO WILHELM VON DER
SCHLICK MEISTER

BRECK GIRL BLISS

Glass

The Cap to a Breck Shampoo Bottle

Ingredients

3 PARTS Light Rum (in a shiny bottle so you can admire your beautiful hair in the reflection)

1 PART White Port (provides the daily vitamins essential for healthy hair follicles)

1 PART Lemon Juice (to amplify the shimmer of your hair)

4 PARTS Sugar Syrup (provides nutrients for the healthy exfoliation of your scalp)

1 Egg White (provides protein essential for strong roots)

Instructions

First, check your hair in the mirror to make sure it's beautiful. (If it's not exactly perfect by Breck girl standards, command your legion of metrosexual campaign hairstylists to apply clouds of hairspray, purifying agents, follicle enhancements, and styling gels.) Next, combine ingredients in a cocktail shaker, adding the egg white at the end and shaking until frothy. Pour into the cap of a Breck shampoo bottle and consume while sobbing for the millions of American children who are starving because of Republicans, yet don't spend a dime of your own $20 million fortune to help them.

Origin

Also known as an "Ambulance Chaser," this adult beverage is named in honor of former senator John Edwards, Democrat vice presidential candidate also known among dittoheads as "the Breck Girl" because of his beautiful, shiny, perfect, All-American hair.

Special Note

According to John Edwards, "when John Kerry is president, people like Christopher Reeve are going to walk again." What he needed to promise was that bald people would grow hair again. "Vote for John Kerry and you'll have wonderful Breck girl hair like mine!" (Then maybe even Dick Cheney would've voted for John F-ing Kerry!)

PELOSI PAINKILLER

Glass

A Democratic National Committee Coffee Mug

Ingredients

1 PART Rum (which also doubles as a handy fuel for hybrid eco-cars)

1 PART Pineapple Juice (in support of the alternative fruit lobby)

1 PART Coconut Cream (plucked from the lush palms surrounding Club G'itmo)

A SPLASH of Orange Juice (provided by Florida Democrats still confused after the 2000 election)

A SPRINKLE of Nutmeg (obtained via a government "nutmeg for the poor" program)

Instructions

While listening to Nancy Pelosi and her liberal friends blame George W. Bush for every evil ever perpetrated on the face of the earth, combine ingredients in a shaker with ice, and shake well. Top off with a sprinkle of nutmeg and consume while providing tax loopholes for the ever-booming California plastic surgery trade.

Origin

This adult beverage is named in honor of House Minority Leader Nancy Pelosi, a wealthy San Francisco elitist Democrat who constantly lectures Americans on the many evils of George W. Bush and his nefarious friends. (This adult beverage is also known as the primary pain reliever proposed by Hillary's Healthcare Task Force).

Special Note

According to Nancy Pelosi, Bush lied because "there's no connection between 9/11 and the war in Iraq." But then other liberal kooks tell us that Bush (along with the CIA) orchestrated 9/11 to create a reason for invading Iraq so as to enrich Halliburton and "big oil." Isn't that a connection? Which one is it? These Democrats need to get better at coordinating their talking points.

FLIP-FLOPPER FIZZ

Glass

Any *Two* Champagne Glasses

Ingredients

2 PARTS Chilled Champagne (although sparkling wine has its good points as well)

2 PARTS Chilled Orange Juice (however, apple juice is also a great option in its own right)

Instructions

While waiting for John Kerry to finish debating himself (a process which may last until the end of time), add some random combination of ingredients to any number of ever-changing drinking containers. Enjoy while watching John Kerry leave the stage of the presidential debates so that he can go sit down among the audience of undecideds. After all, he's sophisticated, intellectual,

and "open-minded" enough to see the merits of voting for
George W. Bush.

Origin

This adult beverage is named in honor of former Democrat
presidential candidate John F-ing Kerry, also known as the
"flip-flopper" for his propensity to simultaneously take every
conceivable position on each and every issue.

> "I actually did vote for the $87 billion, before I voted
> against it."
> —JOHN F. KERRY

LAURA'S LIMEADE

Glass

A "Bush 2004" Souvenir Martini Glass

Ingredients

1 PART Gin (from the liquor cabinet of a big-oil executive board room in Texas)

2 PARTS Lime Juice (example of corporate America's exploitation of scarce lime resources)

A DASH of Triple Sec (part of a Laura Bush–Halliburton profiteering conspiracy)

A DASH of Sugar (part of a Bush bribe from evil sugar plantation owners and "big sugar")

1 Egg White (of which inclusion in this recipe is part of a racist Republican ploy)

Instructions

While Teresa Heinz Kerry chastises Laura Bush for having "never had a real job," conveniently forgetting Laura's years as a librarian, mother of two, and first lady of the United States, combine ingredients in a shaker with ice. Shake well, and pour into a "Bush 2004" souvenir martini glass. Consume while formulating any wacko conspiracy theory involving the Bush family, the CIA, bin Laden, and/or corporate America (unless said theory appeared in Michael Moore's *Fahrenheit 9/11*, in which case it's not a theory, but an absolute fact).

Origin

This adult beverage is named in honor of First Lady Laura Bush, who, despite her spotless image and unblemished reputation, is known to the fringe kook Left only as the wife of evil Hitler clone George W. Bush.

Special Note

According to the liberal mainstream media, Hillary Clinton (not the lovely and gracious Laura Bush) is the perfect illustration of a cookie-baking, nonjudgmental housewife desirous only of world peace — as opposed to Republican women like Laura Bush, Ann Coulter, and Condoleezza Rice, all of whom are fascist, homophobic warmongers who want to burn black churches and kill children by polluting water.

OLD-FASHIONED GRAVITAS

Glass

An "I've Got Gravitas!" Coffee Mug (autographed by Dick Cheney)

Ingredients

1 PART Bourbon (consumed by rugged cowboy types)

1 White Sugar Cube (a potent source of energy enabling round-the-clock gravitas projection)

A DASH of Orange Bitters (representative of liberal media hacks who regurgitate Democrat talking points)

SEVERAL DASHES of "Gravitas"

Instructions

While analyzing a poll that shows 90% of Democrat voters think that Dick Cheney is the name of the latest generic knockoff of Viagra, place the sugar cube in your "I've Got Gravitas!" coffee mug and add bourbon. After swirling the two together, add ice along with a dash of orange bitters. Serve with a strip of orange zest on the side. If you're a member of the liberal media, consume this adult beverage while reading the Democrat talking points for the 2000 presidential campaign (i.e. proclaim Dick Cheney has "gravitas" and then pretend it was your own original thought to say so).

Origin

This adult beverage is named in honor of Dick Cheney, current vice president of the United States and the only human being ever documented to exude a never-ending stream of "gravitas" (a Bush administration "strategery" used to continually defeat Democrats). It is best sipped at an undisclosed location.

Special Note

Given the immense "gravitas" added to the ticket by Dick Cheney's nomination, why was the liberal mainstream media so surprised that Algore and John F-ing Kerry lost? They should be amazed it was even close!

MANHATTAN CARPETBAGGER

Glass
A New York Yankees Sports Bottle Cynically Displayed by Hillary Clinton

Ingredients

1 PART Sweet Vermouth (reminds Hillary of her beloved hometown, Chappaqua)

3 PARTS Rye Whiskey (reminds Hillary of her beloved hometown, Little Rock)

A DASH of Angostura Bitters (reminds Hillary of her beloved hometown, Chicago)

1 Vacant House in the Suburbs

Instructions
First, identify a state where a senator is retiring and move there so you can run for his seat. Next, combine ingredients in a Yankees sports bottle and shake convincingly while pretending to be a lifelong Yankees fan, despite the fact that

long ago you told the entire world your favorite team is the Chicago Cubs.

Origin

This official dittohead adult beverage is named in honor of Hillary Rodham Clinton, resident of Arkansas, Illinois, and Washington, DC, who awoke one day to find herself magically transformed into a senator from New York, no doubt, the result of a vast right-wing conspiracy.

Special Note

With her extensive experience in real estate (renting out the Lincoln Bedroom), cattle futures (turning a $100,000 profit on a thousand bucks in a single day), and publishing (a $7 million book advance), one wonders if Hillary wouldn't be better off pursuing a career as an entrepreneurial capitalist dittohead in the private sector instead of serving as a liberal senator from New York.

PUFF THE MAGIC DASCHLE

Glass

A "Tom Daschle Show" Coffee Mug (guaranteed to put you to sleep)

Ingredients

1 PART Coffee (to wake up Bush voters who kept electing a liberal obstructionist)

1 PART Irish Whiskey (coupled with a Tom Daschle speech, this will put you to sleep)

100 PARTS Partisan Obstructionism (relayed by Daschle in a soft, muted kitten voice)

Instructions

While trying to figure out how the same group of voters can elect both Tom Daschle and George W. Bush by 20-point margins, combine ingredients in a "Tom Daschle Show" coffee mug, and stir gently while puffing on the cigar or cigarette of your choice. Consume this adult beverage while

Tom Daschle accuses you of threatening his family because Rush Limbaugh's venomous hate speech made you do it.

Origin

This adult beverage is named in honor of the rabidly partisan, obstructionist former Senate Minority Leader Tom Daschle (defeated in his 2004 re-election bid), also known among dittoheads as "El Diablo" and "Puff Daschle."

> "What happens when Rush Limbaugh attacks those of us in public life is that people aren't satisfied just to listen. They want to act because they get emotionally invested. And so, you know, the threats to those of us in public life go up dramatically, on our families and on us, in a way that's very disconcerting."
> —TOM DASCHLE

TED "THE SWIMMER" KENNEDY'S BOSTON SOUR

Glass
An Oversized Round Snifter

Ingredients

1 PART Vodka (Ted Kennedy's favorite food group—except Scotch)

1 PART Triple Sec (Ted Kennedy's third favorite food group)

1 PART Sour Mix (which Ted would probably skip, due to its lack of alcohol)

0 Parts Club Soda (water is a phobia of Ted "The Swimmer" Kennedy)

Instructions
Pour equal parts of the above ingredients (so as to maintain a consistent socialist philosophy) into the snifter and consume with breakfast. In the absence of a snifter, pour the concoction into an empty bottle wrapped in a brown paper bag (similar to the ones used by homeless people paid to vote Democrat by MoveOn.org).

Origin

This adult beverage is named in honor of Massachusetts senator Ted "The Swimmer" Kennedy—also known among dittoheads as "The Philanderer." It is also referred to as "Sexual Harrassment on the Beach."

Special Note

Although most dittoheads consume adult beverages in moderation, Ted "The Swimmer" Kennedy's Boston Sour federally mandates the use of portions that may prove fatal to most normal individuals.

THE COWBOY

Glass

A Collectible John Wayne Highball Glass

Ingredients

3 PARTS Rye Whiskey (the kind irresponsibly consumed by out-of-control cowboys)

1 PART Light Cream (yet another Bush link to the infamous Yale Skull & Bones Society)

SEVERAL Ice Cubes (the acquisition of which is the real reason Bush invaded Iraq)

A DASH of Karl Rove (whose name starts with a K...just like the Klan)

1 Harvard MBA (miraculously procured by an idiot frat boy with an IQ of 12)

Instructions

While smearing President Bush as a "cowboy" and "moron" (despite the fact that he's beaten the Democrats in every election and public policy battle since entering politics), mix ingredients in a cocktail shaker and shake vigorously until a frost forms. Pour into a John Wayne highball glass, and consume while proclaiming that even if George W. Bush discovered a cure for cancer, you'd still hate his guts.

Origin

This adult beverage is named in honor of the 43rd president of the United States, George W. Bush, a man dismissed by the Left as nothing more than a hick "cowboy," yet nevertheless maintaining his status among their ranks as the most dangerous threat to world peace since Adolf Hitler (who was a mere choir boy compared to Bush).

Special Note

Is it just a coincidence that every Republican since Watergate has been portrayed as either "stupid," a warmonger "cowboy," or both by the liberal media? Ford was stupid. Reagan was a stupid cowboy. Quayle was stupid. George W. Bush is a stupid cowboy, despite holding a Yale degree and a Harvard MBA. Meanwhile, Algore failed out of seminary and dropped out of law school, yet maintains his status as "a man of brilliance" among the media elite!

BYRD BRAIN

Glass

The Chalice of the Grand Wizard of the Ku Klux Klan

Ingredients

2 PARTS Crème de Banane (the one-time consumption of which was a mistake of Robert Byrd's youth)

1 PART Crème de Cacao (provides strength for droning on incessantly on the Senate floor)

1 PART Light Cream (Robert Byrd prefers light-colored cream)

25 PARTS Blatant Media Hypocrisy (necessary to tolerate a former Klansman as a U.S. senator)

Instructions

While claiming Martin Luther King, Jr. was a troublemaker (which Robert Byrd did) and while using the "N-word" in a television interview (which Robert Byrd also did), pour the ingredients over ice in a cocktail shaker and shake vigorously until frosty. Consume while marveling at the fact that the liberal mainstream media labels conservative Republicans such as Trent Lott "intolerant," while Robert Byrd's real-life membership in the KKK goes completely ignored.

Origin

This adult beverage is named in honor of West Virginia senator Robert Byrd—also known among dittoheads by the name Robert "Sheets" Byrd—Democrat expert on history, rules, and procedure of not only the U.S. Senate but also the West Virginia chapter of the Ku Klux Klan. This adult beverage is also known as "Three Sheets to the Wind."

Special Note

If you're a Republican, do your best to refrain from using this adult beverage to toast the retirement of Strom Thurmond. However, if you're a Democrat, feel free to consume this adult beverage at any Klan rally or "white-only" golf course without fear of repercussion from the liberal mainstream media.

JUMPIN' JIM JEFFORDS

Glass
Any Two Glasses (assuming you switch between the two)

Ingredients:

2 PARTS Vodka (although gin might have better polling numbers)

1 PART Champagne (unless red wine helps further your languishing career)

1 PART Sour Mix (representing the mood of Vermont Republicans who voted for Jim Jeffords)

4 PARTS Sprite (manufactured by a John F-ing Kerry "Benedict Arnold" corporation)

Mexican Jumping Beans (a gift from illegitimately elected former Senate leader Tom Daschle)

Instructions
If you can manage to avoid flipping to another page, combine ingredients in any chilled glass and switch to an entirely new glass before you finish consumption of your adult beverage.

Origin

This adult beverage is named in honor of the independently "moderate" (i.e. "liberal") senator from Vermont, Jim Jeffords, who switched party affiliation in spring 2001, turning control of the Senate over to Tom Daschle and his obstructionist Democrat cohorts.

Special Note

George W. Bush gets more electoral votes than Algore and has an "illegitimate" presidency, but Jumpin' Jim Jeffords (voted into office as a Republican) switches parties right after his election and Tom Daschle doesn't become the "illegitimately elected" Senate majority leader? You just caught a glimpse into the twisted mentality of the liberal mainstream media elite.

VII

THESE ADULT BEVERAGES
HAVE BEEN APPROVED
BY THE UN

COMMIE LIB COOLER

Glass

A Former Soviet Union Official State-Issued Collins Glass

Ingredients

2 PARTS Russian Vodka (purchased during Bill Clinton's 1968 spring break trip to Moscow)

1 PART Kahlua (a bit expensive due to price-gouging Kahlua corporations)

1 Maraschino Cherry (to commemorate the formerly fierce Red Menace)

1 Endless Stream of Liberal Feel-Good Solutions

Instructions

While protesting conservative Republicans' stubborn refusal to drop dead (you'd think at least a few would assume room temperature in an effort to "reach out" in a bipartisan manner), combine ingredients in equal parts (so

as to maintain a rigid adherence to the socialist philosophy) in a former Soviet Union official state-issued Collins glass. Garnish with a cherry, and sip alongside the arts & croissant crowd while advocating liberal feel-good solutions and labeling yourself "progressive."

Origin

This special-edition dittohead adult beverage is named in honor of commie libs, a subspecies of socialists in danger of extinction (many members use their chameleon-like abilities to hide out among the ranks of the environmentalist wackos).

Special Note

Be sure to serve this drink to your guests in equal portions. However, you may dip up as much as you wish for yourself, since you took the time and effort to redistribute the ingredients in a just fashion.

FRENCH MARTINI
ON THE CHIRACS

Glass
An Empty French Wine Bottle

Ingredients

2 PARTS Chambord (a trendy French beverage favored by
Hollywood libs)

1 PART Grand Marnier (a thoughtful appeasement gift for
imperialist foreign dictators)

2 PARTS Orange Juice (selected following a "global taste test"
administered by the UN)

1 PART Soda Water (commonly found in elitist, snobby,
French-looking adult beverages)

1 Maraschino Cherry (harvested under the auspices of the
UN Oil-for-Food program)

Instructions

While staging a pretend election victory party with foreign
leaders who wish John Kerry (the French-looking candidate)
was president (i.e. Jacques Chirac, Kim Jong Il, Osama bin

Laden, and the ayatollahs of Iran), combine ingredients in a shaker with ice, and shake well while demanding that the dwindling relevance of your pathetic nation be recognized by the world's major powers. Consume while reminiscing over liberal mainstream media exit polls that showed John F-ing Kerry taking Texas in a landslide victory with 167% of the vote to George W. Bush's negative 812%.

Origin

This adult beverage is named in honor of France, a devoted socialist utopian ally with a penchant for surrendering to foreign dictators. Also known among dittoheads as the birthplace of freedom fries and the American boycott on French wine.

Special Note

Perhaps Jane Fonda will marry Alec Baldwin, join the Dixie Chicks, and become a citizen of Jacques Chirac's France (along with Barbra Streisand and countless other Hollywood leftists), where they can rest assured that they'll never again face the embarrassing trials and tribulations imposed by living in a nation with a competent and victorious military.

DEAD WHITE GUY GINGER ALE

Glass

A Clay Bowl Stolen from Native Americans (by dead white conquistadors)

Ingredients

1 PART Vodka (a colorless ingredient symbolizing white European oppression)

3 PARTS Ginger Ale (containing blood-thirsty, intolerant, white supremacist sugar)

A SPLASH of White Wine (reminiscent of Napoleonic French imperialism)

A SPLASH of Lemon-Lime Juice (made from fruit hand-picked by indentured servants)

A DASH of Sugar (due to safety concerns, no brown sugar allowed)

Instructions

While attending a college seminar on multiculturalism, with an emphasis on Native American, Afrocentric lesbian poetry, combine ingredients in a clay bowl stolen from Native Americans. Consume on Columbus Day while attacking white males who have the audacity to continue to breathe.

Origin

This adult beverage is named in honor of Christopher Columbus—a capitalist European bigot responsible for the death and murder of eighty trillion pacifist, nature-loving Native Americans (and a man whose lone accomplishment was the "discovery" of someone else's backyard).

Special Warning

Under no circumstances should you add brown sugar to this adult beverage, as it is sure to be ravaged and destroyed by the racist, imperialist, homophobic white sugar already present in the ginger ale.

GRAPE GORBASM

Glass

An Arts & Croissant Crowd–Type Champagne Flute

Ingredients:

1 PART Russian Vodka (in widespread abundance now that capitalism rules Russia)

1 PART Grape Juice (to replenish one's strength following a Gorbasm)

2 PARTS Sour Mix (symbolic of the Gorbasmic liberal disposition toward conservatives)

"The Gorbasm Update Theme" (indistinguishable from Darth Vader's Theme)

Instructions

While waiting patiently for the highly anticipated arrival of Mikhail Gorbachev (as "The Gorbasm Update Theme" plays softly in the background), combine ingredients in a liberal arts & croissant crowd–type champagne flute. Consume while watching liberal elitists burst into collective, spontaneous gor-basm at the mere mention of Mikhail Sergevich Gorbachev.

Origin

This adult beverage is named in honor of the gorbasm—a fake and phony feeling of bliss, euphoria, excitement, ecstasy, and nirvana felt when pondering all the wonderful things that have been done for the planet by Mikhail Gorbachev.

Special Note

This adult beverage is best enjoyed while engaging in a raucous, collective "gorgy" with Phil Donahue, pointy-headed liberal professors from academia, socialist Democrat congressmen, and journalistic members of the sacrosanct media elite.

CLUB G'ITMO GUZZLER

Glass

A Jihad Java Café Coffee Mug (for Koran-compliant non–adult beverages)

Ingredients:

3 PARTS Pineapple Juice (hand-squeezed by attentive butlers)

1 PART Coconut Juice (plucked from the supple palms lining the beaches of G'itmo Bay)

1 PART Lime Juice (left over from the daily full-service continental Islamic breakfast)

A DASH of Sugar Syrup (a Club G'itmo specialty served with an entrée of lemon-baked fish)

1 Club G'itmo Koran (pre-approved by genuine mullahs to be of only the finest quality)

1 Club G'itmo Prayer Rug (in a style that comple-ments the motif of each cell)

Instructions

While enjoying the air-conditioned comfort of Club G'itmo (your tropical retreat from the stress of jihad), combine ingredients in a Jihad Java Café coffee mug and consume while wearing your Club G'itmo T-Shirt at the local Starbucks (where you're sure to be confronted by an angry liberal). Enjoy while watching the latest episode of Robin Leach's *Lifestyles of the Rich & Famous* as he tours the palatial resting quarters of Club G'itmo's most notable and talked-about terrorists.

Origin

This adult beverage is named in honor of the U.S. military detention facility at Guantanamo Bay, known among dittoheads as Club G'itmo. Democrat senator Dick Durbin described it as a "gulag" reminiscent of Nazi death camps, despite the fact that Sunday dinner consists of "orange-glazed chicken, fresh fruit roupee, steamed peas and mushrooms, and rice pilaf." Meanwhile, feeding the terrorists MREs, the standard fare for troops in the field, is strictly forbidden and considered "abusive torture."

POINTY-HEADED PINEAPPLE PROFESSOR PUNCH

Glass

Any Glass Made from Wholly Recycled Materials (must be EPA-approved)

Ingredients

2 PARTS White Wine (a fine European beverage ignored by the crude American proletariat)

2 PARTS Pineapple Juice (made by utopian islanders conquered by American colonialism)

1 PART Carbonated Water (another superior beverage rejected by crass, unrefined Americans)

40 PARTS Leftist Propaganda (otherwise known as "fact" by mainstream media outlets)

1 Liberal, Socialist, Tree-Hugging, Radical, Hippie, Elitist Professor

A LOT of Hot Air (if global warming exists, this is probably why)

Instructions

While being lectured by a long-winded liberal college professor, combine ingredients in a glass of your choice, as long as it is made from wholly recycled materials, because America's depraved capitalistic system is quickly leading us toward an environmental Armageddon of global warming (or cooling, depending on which pointy-headed elitist professor you consult), boiling oceans, and laser-like sun rays that will soon kill us all if we don't follow the enlightened ways of the ivory tower demigods.

Origin

This adult beverage is named in honor of liberal pointy-headed elitist professors from leftist academia whose sole purpose in life is to imbue young skulls full of mush on college campi (that's the EIB plural of campus, for those of you in Rio Linda) across the Fruited Plain with socialist propaganda and anti-capitalist jargon.

Special Note

Used for its intended purpose, this adult beverage will act as a sedative for anyone unfortunate enough to be subjected (most likely against their will) to the droning left-wing lectures of a pointy-headed elitist college professor.

VIII

PMS-NBC vs. FOX News: Old Media vs. New

DAN'S DECEIT

Glass

A "Rather Biased" Coffee Mug

Ingredients

1 PART Rum (is it really rum? Perhaps it's whiskey or a moonshine forgery)

2 PARTS Jack Daniel's (assuming adult beverage experts can verify its authenticity)

1 Liberal Kook (with a history of mental illness and a vendetta against George W. Bush)

A BUNCH of Freepers (each of whom Dan Rather wishes would die a horrible death)

Instructions

While laughing hysterically as Dan Rather lashes out at FOX News Channel and Internet bloggers who have the audacity to point out evidence of his blatant liberal bias, mix ingredients in a Rather Biased coffee mug. Entertain yourself by sipping this adult beverage as Dan Rather insists he's not biased, despite his continued demand that President Bush answer the nevertheless "serious" charges brought up by the *60 Minutes II* memo forgeries.

Origin

This adult beverage is named in honor of Dan Rather's sure to be Emmy Award–winning *60 Minutes II* exposé on President Bush's National Guard service, a story that relied on the word of well-known liberal kook Bill Burkett and a set of forged documents so obviously fraudulent that television viewers uncovered them as forgeries within seven seconds.

Special Note

Dan Rather (also known among dittoheads as "Dan Blather") now says he'd like to "break the story" on how he got his own forged memos! Perhaps his forged documents are the same documents Sandy Berger stuffed in his pants and socks at the National Archives?

INFO-BABE INSANITY

Glass

A Champagne Glass Emblazoned with the Playboy Bunny

Ingredients

4 PARTS Brandy (transforms Uglo-American reporter-ettes into info-babes)

3 PARTS Light Rum (effective in winning over info-babes of the Jamaican persuasion)

1 PART Green Curacao (symbolizing the envy Uglo-Americans harbor toward info-babes)

1 PART Lemon Juice (a vitamin source that gives info-babe skin its beauty)

0 PARTS Prune Juice (symbolizing older female journalists, often replaced by info-babes)

Instructions

While ogling an autographed picture of your favorite info-babe (who became a journalist so she could "change the world"—rather than "report the news"), combine ingredients in a Champagne glass emblazoned with the Playboy bunny. Consume while watching your favorite info-babes on CNN (Clinton News Network), PMS-NBC, or SeeBS Evening news. Finally, marvel in disbelief as the mainstream media lectures the rest of us on the evils of age discrimination as they diligently replace their aging female anchors with younger, more aesthetically pleasing info-babes.

Origin

This adult beverage is named in honor of info-babes: television journalists and commentators of the female persuasion who exhibit certain physical characteristics deemed desirable by society at large (characteristics politically incorrect to point out).

Special Note

Although it may not be politically correct to say so, the truth is that those women labeled by dittoheads as info-babes are in fact "babes" (and are never to be confused with "Uglo-American women").

COCO LOCO CARVILLE

Glass

A Shaved Coconut Shell (to replicate the topography of James Carville's bald head)

Ingredients

1 PART Gin (the adult beverage, not the card game, for those of you in Rio Linda)

1 PART White Rum (a provocative ingredient sporting obvious Republican racial overtones)

2 PARTS White Tequila (imported from socialist Spain)

2 PARTS Pineapple Juice (part of a vast right-wing conspiracy)

1 PART Sugar Syrup (harvested from the Louisiana bayou, home of James Carville)

A SPLASH of Lime Juice (part of yet another vast right-wing conspiracy)

Instructions

While listening to James Carville and liberal Democrats equate Saddam Hussein's mass graves and genocide with the "bag-on-the-head" Abu Ghraib scandal, combine ingredients in a shaved, halved coconut shell. Consume while James Carville defends Bill Clinton for pointing his finger and proclaiming "I did not have sexual relations with that woman!" because, at the time, Bill thought reporters were referring to Hillary, not Monica—so technically, he didn't lie.

Origin

This adult beverage is named in honor of former Clinton campaign aide and current liberal commentator James Carville, known best for his Cajun accent and endless yapping. James is also husband to the lovely and gracious Mary Matalin, an evil Bush administration operative!

Special Note

Did John F-ing Kerry really win the election, only to have it stolen via a Karl Rove–inspired Republican conspiracy? Maybe... Democrat voters are so gullible that James Carville can make an excellent case John F-ing Kerry would've won the election had millions of his supporters not fallen for the "Republicans vote on Tuesday, Democrats vote on Wednesday" parody e-mail.

THE HANNITIZER

Glass

A Ted Kennedy–Sized Bottle of Bourbon (nothing short of a gallon will suffice)

Ingredients

1 BOTTLE of 100 Proof Grain Alcohol (a Ted Kennedy favorite)

1 Copy of Sean Hannity's Deliver Us From Evil

Instructions

While reading a copy of Sean Hannity's book *Deliver Us From Evil* (a reference to both liberals and terrorists), empty a Ted Kennedy–sized bottle of bourbon into the sink because the bourbon isn't strong enough. Next, refill the bottle with 100 proof grain alcohol, and drink the entire concoction in a five-second guzzle. This will replicate both the sensation of a long-time liberal being instantly Hannitized as well as the normal beginning of a day in the life of Ted Kennedy (Warning: Do not actually try this at home. Ted Kennedy is a professional, and amateurs who attempt to emulate him risk severe injury or possible death).

Origin

This adult beverage is named in honor of Sean Hannity, one-time guest host of the show in Rush's absence before hosting his own popular nationally syndicated radio program (as well as FOX News Channel's *Hannity & Colmes*).

Special Note

This adult beverage recipe is meant to be humorous. Therefore, it is recommended that you do not actually consume an entire bottle of grain alcohol in one sitting, much less in a single gulp. This should be blatantly obvious to anyone with half a brain. (However, I'm sure that as you read this, a plethora of liberal Democrat trial lawyers are combing the pages of this book and formulating a multimillion dollar negligence lawsuit.)

WIFE-TRAINING WALTER

Glass

A Wine Glass (brought to you by your wife as you smoke a fine cigar)

Ingredients

1 PART Red Wine (Professor Walter E. Williams's adult beverage of choice)

1 Complacent, Obedient Wife (if you're fortunate enough to have one)

1 Pair of Golf Shoes (so your wife doesn't slip and fall while washing your car)

1 La-Z-Boy Recliner (for relaxing while your wife performs a list of chores)

1 Vacuum Cleaner and/or Kitchen Appliance (an anniversary present for your wife)

Instructions

Have your wife (between doing your laundry and polishing your golf clubs) pour several ounces of your favorite wine into a wine glass and then bring the glass to you on a hand-made silk pillow. Next, provide your wife with a pair of golf shoes so she doesn't slip on the icy driveway while washing your car in the dead of winter. As she washes your car, consume your adult beverage while watching football (preferably a Pittsburgh Steelers game) from the confines of your La-Z-Boy recliner.

Origin

This adult beverage is named in honor of one of the few guest hosts who comes close to filling El Rushbo's enormous shoes—self-described wife-trainer and George Mason University economics professor Walter E. Williams.

Special Note

For a complete list of Walter E. Williams's tips on properly training your wife, visit his website for "The Good Wife's Guide" (from the May 1955 issue of *Housekeeping Monthly*), which provides such essential lessons as "You have no right to question your husband," "Remember that his topics of conversation are more important than yours," and "A good wife always knows her place."

BOOTLEGGING BROADCAST EXCELLENCE

Glass

A "Limbaugh Institute for Advanced Conservative Studies" Coffee Mug

Ingredients

1 PART Tequila (a flawlessly executed stratagem of liquor taste excellence)

1 PART Jack Daniel's (a whiskey...a legend...a way of life...just like Rush!)

1 PART Southern Comfort (on the cutting edge of liquor evolution)

A SPLASH of Orange Juice (supports Rush's former sponsorship of Florida orange juice)

1 COPY of *The Way Things Ought to Be*

A MULTITUDE of Liberals Desperately Trying to Silence Rush Limbaugh

Instructions

While frantically rereading a copy of Rush's first book, *The Way Things Ought to Be* (before the liberal media demagogues succeed in banning it), combine ingredients in a "Limbaugh Institute for Advanced Conservative Studies" coffee mug (purchased on the unregulated, entrepreneur-friendly oasis known as the Internet—loathed by liberals despite the fact that Algore invented it). Consume while reading the Drudge Report or some other new media outlet now doing the job that mainstream journalists and reporters used to do.

Origin

This adult beverage is named in dishonor of the Fairness Doctrine, a never-ending liberal attempt to silence "the most dangerous man in America" via government-imposed censorship and trampling of the First Amendment.

Special Note

If liberals ever succeed in passing the Fairness Doctrine (also known as the "Hush Rush Law"), do not fear. EIB will live on through an illegal underground satellite network of "Bootlegging Broadcast Excellence."

IX

N ANIMALS WERE HARMED IN THE MAKING OF THESE ADULT BEVERAGES

ENVIRONMENTALIST WACKO WHISKEY

Glass

Your Own Cupped Hands

Ingredients

1 PART Triple Sec (as long as it wasn't made in a wicked corporate factory)

2 PARTS Whiskey (homemade by Sierra Club members in an earth-friendly distillery)

1 PART Grain Alcohol (flammable liquid used by the Earth Liberation Front to burn SUVs)

1 Frozen Pond (the result of any number of man-made environmental catastrophes)

1 Dolphin (the pinnacle of creation, according to environmentalist wackos)

Instructions

First, cut several ice cubes from the surface of a frozen pond (these should be abundant due to the smog effect blocking the sun's rays in preparation for the coming ice age). Avoid using a freezer to produce your ice cubes, because freezers are a capitalist-concocted first cousin of man's worst enemy—the air conditioner. Next, combine ingredients (along with your pond cubes) in your own cupped hands. Don't you dare use a glass instead of your hands, because the process of making glass destroys Mother Earth.

Origin

This adult beverage is named in honor of environmentalist wackos, a fringe movement (not to be confused with serious and responsible ecology-minded people) that believes mankind is the greatest threat to nature, seeks to destroy private property, and longs to establish a socialist regime to impose their nuttiness on the rest of us.

Special Note

For years, environmentalist wackos have told us that dolphins are superior to humans—despite the absence of dolphin highways, libraries, or institutions of higher learning. But for all their supposed brilliance, I challenge any environmentalist wacko to find a dolphin that can make an adult beverage as good as this one!

SPOTTED OWL SLAMMER

Glass

Any Shot Glass (the making of which required a tree to be cut down)

Ingredients

1 PART Yukon Jack (the whiskey of choice for lumberjacks)

1 PART Wild Turkey (another endangered species in need of government protection)

Ice Cubes (a result of the modern-day Ice Age triggered by extinction of the spotted owl)

1 Tiny Umbrella (made from the fallen timber of a fire-cleared rain forest)

"The Timber Update Theme" (guaranteed to drive environmentalist wackos totally nuts)

Instructions

Using a fully loaded 12-gauge potato gun (now that the assault weapons ban has been lifted by George W. Bush's corrupt administration), to hunt spotted owls lurking around your neighborhood, pour ingredients (except the tiny wooden umbrella, for those of you in Rio Linda) into any shot glass that required a tree to be cut down for its manufacture. Top off with the tiny umbrella for decorative effect, and consume while listening to "The Timber Update Theme."

Origin

This adult beverage is named in honor of the spotted owls of Oregon and Washington. In the early 1990s, the environmentalist wacko lobby attempted to shut down a large sector of the timber industry with 4,000 spotted owls as the justification (on the assumption that spotted owls were an endangered species). As it turned out, these spotted owls were abundant and were hardly picky about their trees—some of them even nested in Wal-Mart and K-Mart signs!

ACTUAL RUSH LIMBAUGH QUOTE (SURE TO MAKE LIBERALS AND ENVIRONMENTALIST WACKOS CRINGE)

"If the owl can't adapt to the superiority of humans, then screw it."

GLOBAL WARMING CIDER

Glass

A Styrofoam Cup (causing maximum destruction of the ozone layer)

Ingredients

2 PARTS Apple Liqueur (from the same apples Kathleen Turner claims are killing kids)

1 PART Cinnamon Liqueur (factory-processed for maximum environmental damage)

1 COPY of Algore's Manifesto *Earth in the Balance* (research material for the Unabomber's)

1 Extra Styrofoam Cup (for spewing CFCs into an already polluted atmosphere)

Instructions

Pour ingredients into a saucepan and place the pan on your front sidewalk, where it will be brought to a rapid boil due to the abundance of human-created chemicals destroying the ozone layer. Next, pour the pan's contents into a Styrofoam cup. Enjoy while reading about the evils of the internal combustion engine in Algore's manifesto *Earth in the Balance*, as you watch him drive by in his air-conditioned limousine, escorted by a motorcade of gas-guzzling SUVs.

Origin

This adult beverage is named in honor of global warming, the destruction of the ozone layer, and other evil atrocities brought about by the existence of capitalism, free enterprise, and the Republican Party.

Special Warning

This adult beverage must be consumed quickly, because man has fewer than ten years to change his evil ways and go back to living in caves before his capitalistic creations lead to the melting of the polar ice caps, the boiling of the oceans, and the death of all life on Earth (all attributable to the existence of evil Republicans).

LARRY THE LOBSTER'S LUSCIOUS LEMONADE

Glass

A Small Aquarium or Fishbowl ("aquatic prison" in the liberal lexicon)

Ingredients

2 PARTS Lemon Vodka (to cleanse the palate between tasty bites of fresh-killed lobster)

A SPLASH of Blue Curacao (anathema to the Peace Committee to Save Blue Curacao)

1 PART Sprite (manufactured despite the objections of lime-rights activists)

1 Lobster Dinner (a direct provocation of militant vegetarians everywhere)

1 Cardboard Cut-Out of Mary Tyler Moore (to further frighten the lobster)

Instructions

While watching animal rights wackos gather to protest your fine lobster dinner, combine ingredients in a small aquarium or fishbowl (otherwise referred to as an "aquatic prison" by militant vegan extremists). Add multiple straws for your conservative friends and consume while eating a lobster dinner for no other purpose than to annoy Mary Tyler Moore.

Origin

This adult beverage is named in honor of a lobster from an exclusive Manhattan restaurant. After years of living a pampered lifestyle in the restaurant's lavish aquarium, "Larry the Lobster" went on the auction block. El Rushbo (who wanted to eat Larry) and Mary Tyler Moore (who wanted to "free" Larry) entered into an exciting bidding war before the restaurant proprietors decided to let Larry live.

Special Note

If you happen to be a lobster aficionado (one with an appreciation for fine lobster, for those of you in Rio Linda), the author highly recommends Club G'itmo's five-star dining experience. But be sure to make reservations in advance, as Club G'itmo has a long waiting list of wacko jihadists.

LONG-HAIRED, MAGGOT-INFESTED, DOPE-SMOKING PEACE PANSY PUNCH

Glass
A Teacup Reading "Make Love, Not War" (a peace pansy slogan)

Ingredients

2 PARTS Cold Herbal Tea (expressive of the peace pansy way)

2 PARTS Apple Juice (a peaceful, non-threatening, pacifist beverage)

1 PART Pineapple Juice (manufactured from free-range pineapples)

"The Peace Update Theme" (complete with peace pansy–despised bomb sound effects)

Instructions
While participating in the Fifth Annual Global Chili Cook-Off to End War, Genocide, and Republican Breeding, combine ingredients in a teacup reading "Make Love, Not War." Consume while meditating over your capacity "to care"

and your personal yearning to end the global "cycle of violence." Democrat presidential candidates may want to call for a "global taste test" before committing themselves to consumption of this adult beverage.

Origin

This adult beverage is named in honor of long-haired, maggot-infested, dope-smoking peace pansies — people who participate in activities such as the Great Peace March for Global Nuclear Disarmament, volunteer to be human shields for Saddam Hussein, and cringe at the bomb sound effects embedded in the EIB "Peace Update Theme."

Special Note

Not only is a long-haired, maggot-infested, dope-smoking peace pansy an adult beverage, but it's also the type of guy your daughter is bound to bring home before you finish reading this book.

MILITANT VEGETARIAN VODKA

Glass

A Cup Made from Soy (as long as animal fats are not a component)

Ingredients

1 PART Vodka (brewed by dolphins—the most intelligent mammals on Earth)

1 PART Hot and Spicy V8 (made from all-natural, organically grown, non-animal substances)

1 PART Clamato (for hurling at celebrities who dare to wear real fur)

A PINCH of Horseradish (not made from horses, for those of you in Rio Linda)

A SPLASH of Worcestershire and Tabasco (further fanning the flames of militant vegetarianism)

A DASH of Olive Juice (it's okay to recklessly slaughter innocent olives)

A PINCH of Celery Salt and Black Pepper (manufactured from needlessly murdered celery stalks)

Instructions

While attacking the widow of Dr. Atkins (a Svengali-like

neo-Nazi chicken-killer who tricked millions of Americans) because her husband authored a diet that advocated eating lots of meat (thus pushing the propaganda of cow-killing death squads), combine ingredients in a cup made from soy (an all-natural, environmentally friendly, non-animal fat substitute). Consume while lighting meatpacking plants on fire and setting salt-water lobsters free in a freshwater stream. (This kills them, for those of you in Rio Linda.)

Origin

This adult beverage is named in honor of militant vegetarians across the Fruited Plain. Not to be confused with docile, pacifist vegetarians who mind their own business, militant vegetarians are socialist wackos who see no difference between chicken factories and Nazi death camps.

Special Note

Administrators at PETA would like to inform members of the general public that if they encounter any homeless rats, please bring them to the national PETA headquarters so that a home may be found for them. Don't bother to ask for assistance, just release the homeless rats into the lobby and members of PETA will take it from there.

RAIN FOREST FIZZ

Glass

An Earth-Friendly Clay Dipping Spoon (handmade by
Navajo Indians)

Ingredients

3 PARTS Gin (purchased tax-free from an Indian reservation casino)

3 PARTS Club Soda (a cure for cancer covered up by a big drug
industry conspiracy)

2 PARTS Lemon Juice (extracted from naturally deceased,
organically grown lemons)

50 PARTS "Compassion" and "Caring" for the Rain Forest

1 "Rain Stick" (made by Native Americans from a petrified
cactus cadaver)

Instructions

While meditating and reaching a state of oneness with the cos-
mic vibrations of the rain forest, combine ingredients in a clay
dipping spoon handmade by the Navajo Indians, and stir

gently with your finger. Consume while shaking your rain stick in protest of the fascist destruction of the rain forest.

Origin

This adult beverage is named in honor of the world's constantly depleted rain forests, a perfectly harmonious habitat that harbors the only known cure for cancer (even though we haven't found it yet) and animals that supercede human intelligence (which we also haven't found). The rain forest is also known among dittoheads by its former name: "the jungle."

Special Note

Be wary of purchasing your rain stick from an "earth-friendly" environmentalist wacko retail chain at the mall. Each year, these stores slaughter millions of innocent cacti for their own capitalistic gain. Make sure your rain stick bears the label "Handmade from a Naturally Deceased Cactus."

ANIMAL RIGHTS AFTERGLOW

Glass

A Wineskin Made from Goat

Ingredients

1 PART Gin (only "Beefeater" brand gin will suffice)

1 PART Midori (it's okay to slaughter melons, just not the animals that eat them)

1 PART Blue Curacao (seriously, try it—it tastes just like chicken)

"The Animal Rights Update Theme" (guaranteed to irk liberals everywhere)

Instructions

While throwing blood on a celebrity's fur coat (even if it happens to be fake fur), combine ingredients in a mixing glass. Pour into a wineskin for easy transport and consume while protesting the evil capitalistic exploitation of animals by corporate America, particularly "big ketchup."

Origin

This wonderful adult beverage is named in honor of the animal rights crowd and militant vegetarians everywhere. This is the perfect adult beverage to serve to your dinner party guests, preferably following a main course of steak or chicken.

Enhance your enjoyment of this adult beverage by wearing a "People Eating Tasty Animals" T-shirt.

Special Note

The best wineskins are produced from goatskin, so don't be fooled by a second-rate "pleather" version.

FROG-LICKING WILD RIDE

Glass

A Kermit the Frog Kiddie Cup

Ingredients

1 PART Vodka (kills off unwanted disease-ridden amphibian bacteria)

2 PARTS Lemonade (helps negate the unpopular, non-hallucinogenic frog aftertaste)

1 Frog (for the purpose of recreational licking)

Instructions

First, be sure to have a frog handy and ready to lick. Next, pour ingredients into a Kermit the Frog kiddie cup (the licking of which will NOT result in a drug-induced euphoria). Consume while getting high off frog licks. Me Generation liberals who wish to relive the 1960s are encouraged to lick their frogs while actually riding Disney World's "Mr. Toad's Wild Ride." This will replicate the dope-smoking ecstasy of nostalgic days spent as a long-haired, maggot-infested, dope-smoking peace pansy.

Origin

This adult beverage is named in honor of the Colorado spotted toad, which, if licked, provides a hallucinogenic high. It is intended that this adult beverage will serve as a palate-cleanser between frog licks.

Special Note

Where's PETA? Isn't being licked a violation of the frog's rights? Can a frog legally give its consent to be licked?

SUV ON THE ROCKS

Glass

A Collins Glass Made from a Recycled Economy Car Windshield

Ingredients

2 PARTS Root Beer (an alternative fuel that will power future enviro-friendly cars)

A DASH of Angostura Bitters (symbolizing liberal hatred of SUVs)

1 PART Baileys (a future alternative fuel big oil doesn't want you to know about)

ICE CUBES (certain to melt from the noxious carbon emissions belched out by your SUV)

1 Evil, Gas-Guzzling Death Machine

Paul Shanklin's Musical Parody "In a Yugo" (in which Elvis sings of the dangers of liberalism)

Instructions

While revving the engine of your SUV (in a premeditated

conspiracy to pollute and destroy the planet), combine ingredients in a Collins glass (preferably one manufactured from the recycled, steamrolled windshield of a tiny "fuel-efficient" economy car). Consume while listening to Paul Shanklin's musical parody "In a Yugo" on your SUV's CD player.

Origin

Created in honor of the interest group "Citizens for Vehicle Choice," this adult beverage is named for the one thing on Earth that may be worse than smoking a cigarette—driving an SUV.

Special Warning

Under no circumstances should you drink this adult beverage while driving your SUV, as it will increase the likelihood of your SUV participating in a wild and unprovoked killing spree followed by subsequent headlines such as "Drunken SUV Kills Five," "Police Arrest SUV for DUI," or "SUV Caught Driving While Intoxicated."

ACKNOWLEDGMENTS

Special thanks to Kit Carson and David Limbaugh, without whom this book would not have been possible. I would also like to thank God, Jen, my parents, Ryan and Sara Farish, the staff at Regnery, and all of my friends and family who helped see this book through its long and arduous journey to print.

INDEX

ALPHABETICAL LIST OF ADULT BEVERAGES

Get a FREE chapter
of Regnery's latest bestseller!

Visit us at

www.Regnery.com

- Hot New Releases

- Upcoming Titles

- Listings of Author Signings
  and Media Events

- Complete Regnery Catalog

- Always a Free Chapter
  of a Brand-New Book!

Since 1947
**REGNERY
PUBLISHING, INC.**
An Eagle Publishing Company • Washington, DC
www.Regnery.com